MW01236363

 Special Gift

For _Alexander_
Sunshine

From _MaMaw Wetheyholt_

On _Dec. 24, 1993_

"Jesus loves the little children
of the world."

Dedicated in loving memory
to
my dear friend, Mrs. Helen Doyle
whose love for Jesus was reflected in a
lifetime of nurturing scores of children,
which she took in and raised as her
very own, under one of the happiest
roofs in Western Colorado.

ISBN 0-529-10003-7
Copyright © 1993 Marjorie Decker

Published by
WORLD BIBLE PUBLISHERS, INC.
1500 Riverside Drive, Iowa Falls, IA 50126

CHRISTIAN MOTHER GOOSE®

Rock-A-Bye
Stories of Jesus

Selected Scripture from
The Authorized King James Version

Written and Illustrated
by
Marjorie Ainsborough Decker

CONTENTS

CONTENTS

TELL ME
THE STORIES OF JESUS

Tell me the stories of Jesus,
Tell me a story each day;
How He came down from Heaven;
How He was born in the hay.

Stories about the fishes;
Stories about the sea;
How He could walk on the water;
How He made blind eyes to see.

Stories of people who followed;
Stories of five loaves of bread;
How wind and waves obeyed Him.
How He arose from the dead.

Stories about the angels;
Stories about His star;
How He will take me to Heaven;
How many wonders there are!

But these are written, that ye might believe that Jesus is the Christ, the Son of God...
John 20:31

Tell me the stories of children
Crowding around His knee;
Tell me the stories of Jesus;
Stories of how He loves me!

BETHLEHEM BABY

Born in a tiny town:
  Bethlehem Baby.
Leaving His Heavenly Crown;
Who is He? Tell me!

Beautiful Jesus –

Everlasting God –

The Lord of lords –

Heaven 's own Prince –

Love Gift of God –

Earth's own Creator –

Hope of the world –

Eternal Savior –

Messiah and King –

... Jesus was born in Bethlehem ....
Matt. 2:1

Bethlehem, Bethlehem,
His star is shining bright!
Bethlehem, Bethlehem.
God's Son is here tonight!

HOW DID JESUS GET HIS NAME?

"How did Jesus get His Name?"
A small boy asked his Dad.
"Who chose it for Him?
Did He like it? Did it make Him glad?"

"God, His Father, chose His Name,"
The small boy's Daddy smiled;
"He sent an angel with the Name
Especially for this Child."

"Yes, I'm sure He liked His Name,
Because His Father gave it.
His Name means 'Savior,' and He came
Down to this world to save it."

"'Jesus' is His earthly Name,
Because before He came,
All of Heaven knew The Lord
By all His Heavenly Names."

"That's how Jesus got His Name;
The Bible tells us so.
And what a lovely Name it is
For little ones to know."

... thou shalt call His Name JESUS:
Matt: 1:21

JESUS HAD A BED OF WOOD

Jesus had a bed of wood,
    The night that He was born;
Where sheep and cattle 'round Him stood,
    Among the hay and corn.
His bed was called a manger,
    And filled with straw and hay,
Where all the gentle creatures
    Found food there, day by day.

This night, their wooden manger
    Had become a wooden bed,
For a tiny Babe from Heaven,
    Who would feed the world, instead.
The sheep all softly bleated,
    Just as if they understood,
God's own dear Son lay sleeping,
    In that old, rough bed of wood.

As years and years went by,
    Jesus grew so strong and brave;
He always cared about the ones
    He'd come to seek and save.
He called us all His own lost sheep,
    Who couldn't find their way;
And so another bed of wood
    Was made for Him to lay.

He lay, this time, upon a Cross
　　　Made from an old rough tree.
And there He died, because He loved
　　　Those lost sheep – you and me.
But God has written in His Word
　　　How Jesus rose in glory!
He lives in Heaven – and so shall we!
　　　Oh, what a wondrous story:
That such a loving Savior –
　　　God's own Son, so kind and good –
Came to earth one Christmas day,
　　　In a little bed of wood.

MARY'S SONG

If you lived in Bethlehem,
  And passed by Joseph's shop,
You would hear a song at night,
So lovely, you would stop.
    And you'd listen ...
    And you'd listen ...
And you'd wonder who would sing
Such a love song, to a baby;
Even stars are listening ...

    "Little Baby,
    Baby Jesus,
All the world has waited long,
    For Your coming
    Down from Heaven,
So I sing You Mary's Song ...

"You are lovely;
You are holy;
And I'll love You all my days.
And I hold You;
And I rock You;
And I sing to You sweet praise."

 JESUS WAS THERE!

Before the world began –
   Jesus was there!
When Adam was a man –
   Jesus was there!

When Noah's ark set sail –
   Jesus was there!
When Jonah met the whale –
   Jesus was there!

When David drew his sling –
   Jesus was there!
When Esther faced the king –
   Jesus was there!

To make this big round earth –
   Jesus was there!
Before Mary gave Him birth –
   Jesus was there!

*And now, O Father, glorify thou Me with
thine own self with the glory which I had
with thee before the world was.*
John 17:5

FEED MY LAMBS

Feed my lambs,
All the little lambs;
Feed the little lambs
That run and jump and play.
Jesus wants His little lambs
Cared for and fed
On His Living Water,
And His Heavenly Bread.

... He saith unto him, Feed
My lambs. John 21:15

FOLLOWING A STAR

Following a star,
    Following a star,
See the wise men coming!
Riding from afar.
All the way to Bethlehem,
With presents in a jar;
Looking for the little King,
Following a star!

Other people saw
That star in the skies,
But never thought to follow,
Like those who were wise.
When the wise men found the King,
They found the door ajar;
They found the little King by
Following a star!

Where the star led them,
A light leads today,
To Jesus, The King,
Who welcomes you to stay.
He will guide you to His home,
No matter where you are,
Like the wise, wise men of old,
Following a star!

*... For we have seen His star
in the east, and are come to
worship Him. Matt. 2:2*

OLD SIMEON
AND BABY JESUS

Old Simeon came
To the temple one day;
'Twas the day
    He'd been waiting for.
God's Spirit had told him
    That Christ would be there,
So he waited inside the door.

His kindly old face,
    And his gentle old eyes,
Watched the babies
    And parents who came.
And he knew right away,
    When Mary came in,
That "Christ" was her baby's Name.

He took Jesus up
    In his loving old arms,
"Bless The Lord!
    "Bless The Lord!" he cried.
"My old eyes have seen
    The Savior of men;
Take me home, now; I'm satisfied."

*For mine eyes have seen
thy salvation. Luke 2:30*

Old Simeon's face,
    And his gentle old eyes,
Shone with light
    In each wrinkle and crease.
As sweet Baby Jesus
    Looked up with a smile,
That sent Simeon home in peace.

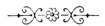

THE LITTLE CARPENTER

Oh, there's a little carpenter,
Who sweeps the shop each day;
He's learning how to polish wood,
And put His tools away.

And He sings at His work;
Yes, He sings, sings, sings!
He's a happy working boy,
And the coming King of kings!

His mother loves the little things
He makes from bits of wood;
And often shares those little gifts
Around the neighborhood.

And He sings at His work;
Yes, He sings, sings, sings!
He's a happy working boy,
And the coming King of kings!

*And the child grew, and waxed
strong in spirit, filled with
wisdom ....   Luke 2:40*

They call Him "Little Jesus",
    Who helps Joseph with a song.
He's willing to obey and learn,
    While growing wise and strong.

    And He sings at His work;
    Yes, He sings, sings, sings!
    He's a happy working boy,
    And the coming King of kings!

WILL HE?

When Mary came to Nazareth,
　Her friends all came to see
The little boy by Joseph's side,
And asked, "What will He be?"

"Will He be a carpenter,
And grow up big and strong?
Or will He be a soldier,
And sing a battlesong?
Will He be a wise boy?
Who brings His mother joy?
Will He be the best friend
Of every girl and boy?
Will He be a kind man,
Who loves the beasts and birds?
Will He be a Teacher,
To teach God's Holy Words?
Will He be a Healer,
To heal the sick and lame?"
"Yes," said Mary, "and much more –
For JESUS is His Name!"

... Jesus of Nazareth, a man approved
of God among you by miracles and
wonders and signs .... Acts 2:22

24

GLOW, GLOW, GLOW!

Here a light! There a light!
Yours and mine.
Little lights for Jesus,
Letting our lights shine!
We'll light up the darkness,
Everywhere we go;
Here a light! There a light!
Glow, Glow, Glow!

Let your light so shine
before men ... Matt. 5:16

GOOD NEWS! GOOD NEWS!

Good News! Good News!
There's Good News everywhere!
For God is good,
And every day
His goodness we all share.

Good News! Good News!
There's Good News everywhere!
For God is good,
And all the world
Is full of wonders fair.

Good News! Good News!
There's Good News everywhere!
For God is good,
And offers all
His love, His Son, His care.

Good News! Good News!
There's Good News everywhere!
For God is good,
And gave His Word;
Oh! Read the Good News there!

*Fear not: for, behold, I bring
you good tidings of great joy,
which shall be to all people.*
Luke 2:10

BENEATH HIS WINGS

When Jesus was a little boy,
  He watched a mother hen
Gathering all her little chicks
Beneath her wings –
    And then ...

When Jesus was a grown-up man,
He watched a certain town,
And cried, in sorrow, to the folk
Who hurried up and down –
    "Jerusalem! Jerusalem!
    How often would I bring
    Your little children unto Me
    to rest beneath My wings!"
    And then ...

Just like a loving mother hen,
He called them to Him, once again.
But they refused and turned away;
Oh, what a sad and sorry day –
    For Jerusalem.

But there's still room
For all to share,
Beneath His wings –
Let's nestle there.

*... How often would I have gathered
thy children together, even as a hen
gathereth her chickens under her
wings.... Matt. 23:37*

LET THE CHILDREN COME TO ME

"Let the children come to Me,
Do not turn one away!"
Jesus said these lovely words,
So every child could stay.
How the children ran to Him,
And jumped upon His knee;
Little faces laughed and smiled,
As He said lovingly:
"Let the children, let the children
        All come unto Me!"

So, a little child like you,
With little hands and feet,
Jesus calls for you to come
Into His arms so sweet.
He will bless and hold you,
You'll be safe as you can be,
With Jesus as your Savior,
Who still says lovingly:
"Let the children, let the children
        All come unto Me!"

... Suffer little children to come unto Me ....
Luke 18:16

A SURPRISE IN THE STORM

The waves of the sea
   Were blown all about;
Blown high by the winds,
   Like a great waterspout!
"My, my!" cried the fishes,
   Tossed up here and there;
"We're meant to be swimming,
   Not flying on air!"

Big turtles and crabs
    Were turned upside down;
The fishermen shouted,
    "Help! Help! or we'll drown!"
But there in the boat,
    Without any fear,
Jesus was sleeping
    As waves pounded near.

The fishermen shouted,
    "Wake up from your sleep,
Or, Master, we'll perish
    In this stormy deep!"
Then Jesus woke up,
    And He spoke to the storm:
"Be still, wind and waves;
    Peace – let there be calm."

At once! Right away!
    And quick as a flash,
The sea was all calm;
    Not even a splash!
The fishes and turtles,
    And crabs blinked their eyes;
The fishermen trembled
    In shock and surprise!

"Why, even the winds
 And the waves must obey,
They do what He tells them;
 And with no delay!"
"Do not be afraid,"
 Jesus said, "Trust in me,"
As onward they sailed
 On the peaceful blue sea.

*And He arose, and rebuked
the wind, and said to the
sea, Peace, be still ...*
Mark 4:39

HEAVENLY SECRETS

Did you know that God has secrets
Just for little children's ears?
They are secrets that some grown-ups
Haven't heard for years and years.

Jesus told us in the Bible,
He was glad that God had kept
Some special Heavenly secrets
For the children to accept.

So, be listening, little children,
For the secrets God will share;
Listen for those Heavenly secrets,
As you talk to Him in prayer.

LOVE ONE ANOTHER

Little children,
    Love one another;
Honor thy father
    And thy mother.
Be ye kind,
    And quick to forgive;
Loving Jesus
    As long as you live.

... We should love one another.
I John 3:11

A PEACEMAKER'S HOUSE

My! What a messy house,"
    Said Tommy Tittlemouse,
As he looked all around his room.
    "I can't have peace and rest,
Until I do my best,
    With soap and water and a broom."

So he scrubbed and he swept,
    Picked up things that he kept
In a closet or in a drawer.
    He found things that were lost,
In some bags that were tossed
    In a corner across the floor.

He washed the window panes,
    Put away books and trains,
And then made his tittlemouse bed.
    When everthing was neat,
He put up his little feet,
    And enjoyed some tittlemouse bread.

A peace now filled each room,
Whisking out untidy gloom,
"Now, my peace I'll share with a guest.
I'm a peacemaker," he said,
As he bowed his little head,
In his house so cozy and blessed.

THE GUEST IN SPARROW'S TREE

"Oh, look! We have a guest today!"
    Said Sparrow to his mate;
"A very large brown guest, I say,
    If judging by his weight!"

"I wonder what he's doing here,
    Up in our family tree.
I think he climbed up here to look
    At all the crowd I see."

"Here's Jesus! We can see Him now!"
    The children shouted loud.
"Aha!" chirped Mrs. Sparrow,
    "He's the reason for this crowd."

Their very large brown guest leaned out,
    Far out upon a limb;
As Jesus walked below the tree,
    He stopped to look at him.

"Zacchaeus, hurry down, because
        Today, I'll be your guest.
Be careful as you're coming down;
        Do not disturb the nest."

The crowd all grumbled and complained,
        "He's going home with him?
That little man, Zacchaeus, needs
        To stay up on that limb."

*... Zacchaeus, make haste, and
come down; for today I must
abide at thy house. Luke 19:5*

"They think our guest is very small;
    That can't be," Sparrow said.
"He's very large, indeed, to us
    And must need lots of bread."

Zacchaeus climbed down from the tree;
    The Lord would be his guest.
He jumped for joy and gladness, while
    The sparrows chirped their best.

They listened as they watched the Lord,
    (Who's kind to little birds)
Walk home with small Zacchaeus, and
    They heard His gentle words.

Their little sparrow hearts were glad
    That, while up in their tree,
Zacchaeus welcomed his own guest
    To dinner, joyfully.

And they that had eaten were about four thousand....
Mark 8:9

ONE LOAF, TWO LOAVES

One loaf, two loaves,
Three loaves, four!
Five loaves, six loaves,
Seven loaves more!
Give them all to Jesus,
And in His loving hand,
Seven loaves will feed
Four thousand children
In the land!

A BLESSING FOR BARTIMAEUS

Poor, blind Bartimaeus,
    He couldn't see the sun;
He couldn't see a rabbit,
    Or watch the children run.

He sat beside the roadway,
    To hear the children play;
And children who were kind,
    Stopped to speak to him each day.

One day, they sang him songs,
    As they played a tambourine;
Then all at once they shouted,
    "Here comes the Nazarene."

When poor, blind Bartimaeus
    Heard Jesus coming by,
His heart was filled with hope
    That The Lord would hear his cry:

"Dear Jesus, please have mercy."
    But many people tried
To tell him to be quiet,
    But he all the louder cried!

So Jesus stopped and asked him,
   "What do you want from Me?"
Blind Bartimaeus answered,
   "Lord Jesus let me see!"
Then Jesus answered, kindly,
   "Go on your way, you're healed."
At once, blind Bartimaeus
   Could see each tree and field!
Oh, happy Bartimaeus!
   With happy children, too,
Followed Jesus down the road,
   As thankful people do!

JEWELS FOR JESUS

Jewels for Jesus!
Jewels for Jesus!
Jewels He bought,
That sparkle and shine!

Jewels that light up
The world for Jesus;
Jewels so precious,
Of every design.

One day He's coming,
His Jewels to take;
He'll call them by name,
With not one mistake!

Then off through the clouds,
His Jewels will fly;
Off to His palace
Way up in the sky.

And there they will shine,
On streets made of gold;
The King's own Treasure,
With value untold!

Jewels for Jesus!
Far richer that pearls –
Are all of His own
Little boys and girls!

KNOCK, KNOCK

Wee Willie Winkie
Ran through the town,
Knocking on a doorway,
In his nightgown:
"Friend, please lend me three loaves,
To feed a midnight guest."
His friend would not get up,
He said, "I've gone to bed to rest."

Knock – knock ...
Knock – knock – knock ...

Knock – knock ...
Knock – knock – knock ...

Wee Willie Winkie
Knocked even more!
"All I need is three loaves,
And not one more."
Because he kept on knocking,
His friend got up and said,
"Come in and take all that you want,
So I can get to bed."

... knock, and it shall be opened unto you.
Luke 11:9

JESUS, TEACH ME
HOW TO PRAY

Jesus, teach me how to pray;
How to love You more each day.
Kind, in what I do and say;
Quick and happy to obey.
Teach me from Your Holy Word,
Lessons from the love You shared.
You have been a child, and know
What is in my heart, and so ...
Jesus, teach me how to pray;
How to love You more each day.

... Lord, teach us to pray ...
Luke 11:1

TWELVE BASKETS OF BREAD

The stars were twinkling brightly,
   On a little, dusty town,
Where, snuggling in his cozy bed,
   A little boy lay down.

And as he lay, he wondered
   All about his happy day;
And how he'd given Jesus
   All his lunch to give away.

And how his little lunch had fed
    Five thousand men, or more.
When Jesus blessed and shared it,
    It kept growing by the score!

And even when the people
    Were all full, and Jesus said,
"Now, gather up the pieces,"
    There was still a mound of bread.

But not a piece was wasted,
    They were gathered up instead,
By all the twelve disciples ...
    Yes! Twelve baskets full of bread!

The little boy had hurried
    All the way back home, and ran
To tell about the miracle,
    And how it all began.

Soon after he arrived there,
    The disciples came to find
The little boy who gave his lunch,
    Who'd been so good and kind.

They gave him all twelve baskets
    Of the bread that Jesus saved;
What a great reward of bread
    From a little lunch he gave.

The people in the village,
    Were amazed at what they heard:
"Five thousand men all eating
    From a lunch blessed by His word."

His mother came and told them,
    "There is bread for everyone;
Run home and bring your basket,
    And we'll pass this blessing on!"

"A miracle from Jesus!
    A miracle we can share,"
The people shouted happily;
    "God bless our neighbor there!"

By nighttime, all the baskets
    Had been shared around the town;
Except the one inside the room
    Where the little boy lay down.

It sat so full beside him,
    In the quiet of his house;
But peeping in the basket
    Was a tiny, hungry mouse.

The little boy spoke softly,
    "Little mouse beside my bed,
I know it pleases Jesus,
    If we share our loaves of bread."

"Since Jesus cares for creatures,
    And the people now are fed;
You, too, can share His goodness
    From this basket full of bread."

So, nibble...nibble...nibble,
    Went the little mouse with joy!
As off to sleep and dreamland,
    Went that happy little boy!

IT'S SO NICE
TO TALK TO JESUS

It's so nice to have a friend
Who will listen while you tell
All that happened through the day,
      And who'll listen very well.

It's so nice when someone's there,
      Who will listen to the end
Of every little story,
      If it's real or just pretend!

It's so nice to have a friend,
      At your home, at school, at play.
You just can't wait to tell them
      All the things you have to say.

It's so nice to talk to Jesus,
      He will listen to the end;
And He will not interrupt you;
      He's your very dearest Friend.

54

OH, AREN'T YOU GLAD!

Oh! aren't you glad that Jesus
   Takes care of little birds;
Of moles, and sheep, and creatures,
   And cattle in their herds.
And if He cares for sparrows,
   When they fall out of a tree,
Your worth is more than sparrows;
   Oh! how special you must be!

*... Fear not therefore: ye are of more
value than many sparrows. Luke 12:7*

RED SKY AT NIGHT

Little Boy Blue;
Come, blow your horn,
Bring in the lambs,
Who hear you warn:

"Red sky at night,
Shepherd's delight;
Red sky at morning,
Shepherd's warning."

Bring in the lambs,
Where they will be warm;
Safe from the rain,
And safe from the storm.

Little Boy Blue,
Come, blow your horn,
Bring in the sheep
From the fields of corn.

Old sheep should know,
When the sky is red,
Signs of a storm
Are over their heads.

"Red sky at night,
Shepherd's delight;
Red sky at morning,
Shepherd's warning."
Little Boy Blue,
Come, blow your horn,
Bring in the sheep
From the fields of corn.

FOUR FAITHFUL FRIENDS

"We must see Jesus,
We must see Him!"
Four men kept shouting so loud.
As they carried a sick man
There on his bed,
But they couldn't
Get through the crowd.

Crowds in the doorway;
Crowds on the stairs;
And crowds all over the house.
There were crowds in the front,
And crowds in the back,
With no space for even a mouse.

'Round and around
Went the sick man's friends.
They wouldn't give up, forsooth!
"If we can't get to Jesus
In front or in back,
We'll get to Him through the roof."

While Jesus preached
In the crowded house,
The friends were struggling outside,
To lift the sick man
Up the stairs to the roof,
"For nothing will stop us," they cried.

Panting for breath,
One step at a time,
The four went up stair by stair.
Those four faithful friends
Were determined to get
Their sick friend
To Jesus down there.

Reaching the top
Of the roof, they tied
Long ropes on the sick man's bed.
Then, up there on the roof,
They made a big hole
Right over the dear Savior's head!

Bits of the roof
Kept falling below,
With dust dropping everywhere.
Looking up, Jesus saw
The sick man's four friends
Drop him down
Through the hole up there.

... they uncovered the roof where He was.
Mark 2:4

Down, down he came,
And Jesus could see
His friends had faith in God's truth.
So He healed the sick man,
Who jumped up for joy!
With cheers from his friends
On the roof!

THE LITTLE MEETING

I held a little meeting
    To sing, and preach and pray.
And do you know how many came
    To join me on that day?

There weren't so very many;
    Just I, myself, and me.
But all of us knew Jesus
    Would join our "little three."

"Myself" did all the preaching,
    As "me" took turns to pray;
And "I" did all the singing,
    Then we closed and went to play.

WALK A MILE WITH ME

Walk a mile, walk a mile,
Walk a mile with me.
Walk a mile, and we will smile
At all the things we see.
Walk a mile? Walk a mile?
Walk a mile with you?
Yes, I'll walk with you a mile;
And not just one, but two!

*And whosoever shall compel thee
to go a mile, go with him twain.*
Matt. 5:41

GENTLE JESUS

Gentle Jesus,
 Always kind;
  Always seeking
  Sheep to find;
Always watching over me;
Always, always loving me;
Gentle Jesus, always true;
Gentle Jesus, I love You!

JESUS LEFT A CLUE

I know I can't see Jesus,
   But I really know He's there.
He left a clue behind Him,
That we all see everywhere!
Just take a look around you,
And His clue is obvious;
His clue will tell you He is real –
         What is it?
         He made Us!

All things were made by Him ...
         John 1:3

LOST AND FOUND

Ninety-nine, ninety-nine,
  Ninety-nine small sheep,
Nibbling on the grassy slope,
    Until it's time to sleep.

Only one, only one,
    Only one lost sheep,
Far away, out in the cold;
    Too afraid to sleep.

Here he comes! Here he comes!
    The kindly Shepherd man;
Looking for that one lost sheep,
    Before the night began.

Only one, only one,
    Only one small cry,
Led the kindly Shepherd
    To the one lost sheep close by.

Here they come! Here they come!
    The Shepherd and the sheep.
Coming home so joyfully
    Back to the Shepherd's keep.

MY VERY OWN LORD'S PRAYER

Our Father, which art in Heaven,
Hallowed be Thy Name ...

> "Excuse me, I just peeked
> and saw my brand new checker game."

Thy kingdom come,
Thy will be done ...

> "Oh, look! A bug jumped on my thumb.
> What's next? Oh, yes" –

In earth as it is in Heaven.

> "Dear God, do angels up in Heaven
> know that tomorrow I'll be seven?"

Give us this day our daily bread ...

> "So I can see the birds are fed."

And forgive us our debts,
As we forgive our debtors ...

> "When John was sorry for the way
> he tore my picture book today,
> I did forgive him, 'cause I knew
> that last week he forgave me, too."

His ears are open unto their prayers. I Pet. 3:12

"Dear Lord, I did learn all the rest;
    let's see ... I'll do my very best ..."
And lead us not into temptation,
But deliver us from evil:
For Thine is the Kingdom,
And the power, and the glory ...
    "It's almost time
    for my 'Jesus Story' ..."
For ever and ever, Amen. "Goodnight ...."

THE LITTLE GIRL'S MIRACLE

As Jesus stepped out of a boat one day,
    And walked on the sands of the shore,
A man called Jairus cried out to the Lord,
"My little girl lies at death's door!
        Come home with me, Jesus,
        Come quickly, now!"
But crowds had all gathered around;
        They pushed and shoved,
        To welcome The Lord;
No way through the crowd could be found.

Before Jesus went on His way again,
A servant came running, and said,
        "Don't trouble the Master,
        It's now too late;
Your dear, only daughter is dead."
At once, Jesus spoke, "Do not be afraid,
Just trust Me, and only believe.
        Your dear little girl
        Shall soon be made well,
So there is no reason to grieve."

At long last they came to Jairus' house,
Where everyone started to weep.
    But Jesus spoke loud,
    To all of them there,
"The child is not dead, she's asleep."
    "Asleep! She's asleep!"
    The weepers now laughed;
They couldn't believe what they heard.
So Jesus sent all of them out of the room,
Except those who trusted His word.

Then, taking the little girl by her hand,
He called, "Little maiden, arise!"
At Jesus' words, the little girl moved,
And stood, as she opened her eyes!
　　Her mother and father
　　Were filled with joy;
They had never heard words so sweet.
　　The Lord Jesus smiled
　　At the happy child,
Then said, "Give her something to eat."

And, oh, how that family loved The Lord;
His words were like living water.
　　They said, "He's our Savior,
　　Our Healer and Friend,
Who gave us our miracle daughter."

*He ... took her by the hand, and called,
saying, Maid, arise.*　　　　*Luke 8:54*

WALKING ON THE WATER

Walking on the water,
Walking on the sea;
Isn't that impossible?
It is to you and me!
Walking on the water,
Walking on the sea;
Jesus took a stroll at night,
As easy as can be!

... Jesus went unto them,
walking on the sea.
Matt. 14:25

THE DAY THAT JESUS WEPT

When Jesus wept,
The angels wept,
To see His teardrops fall.
His friend had died, and so He cried,
Against the gravestone wall.

Amidst His tears,
In front of all,
He said, "Remove this stone!
And you will see God's glory,
By believing Me alone."

Then with a loud
Loud voice, He cried,
"Come! Lazarus. Come out!"
And Lazarus came, all wrapped in cloth;
'Twas Lazarus, there's no doubt!

"Unwrap him now,
And let him go!"
His family then was told;
So they unwrapped their precious gift,
More valuable than gold!

I am the resurrection, and the life: he that believeth in Me, though he were dead, yet shall he live.
John 11:25

Oh, happy day!
Oh, happy day!
God's promise Jesus kept:
He was the Champion over death! ...
The day that Jesus wept.

... Such as hear the word, and
receive it, and bring forth fruit ...
Mark 4:20

DEAR LITTLE SEED

Dear little seed,
     You were meant to be sown
Down in the ground,
        Not stored all alone.
There in the ground,
        You'll put down a good root;
Then soon will appear
        A most beautiful fruit!

Dear little word,
        You were meant to be sown
Down in my heart,
        Not on ground of stone;
There in my heart,
        You'll put down a good root;
Then soon will appear
        God's own beautiful fruit!

JESUS NEVER BREAKS A PROMISE

Jesus never breaks a promise;
  Never, never, never!
You can trust His every word,
Always and forever!
Every promise God has made,
He's trusted to His Son.
Jesus never breaks a promise,
Never! No, not one!

For all the promises of God in
Him are yea, and in Him
Amen ....   II Cor. 1:20

MAKE WAY FOR THE KING!

Make way for the King!
Make way for the King!"
The children shouted loud.
Waving branches in their hands,
Before the cheering crowd.

"Hosanna, we sing!
Hosanna, we sing!
All the way through town.
Jesus has come
In the Name of The Lord!
Make way for The King!
And bow down."

STONE, STONE ROLL AWAY!

"Stone, stone roll away,
This is Resurrection Day!"
God's angel sang, then, all alone,
Rolled back the tomb's
Great, heavy stone!
He sat upon the top to sing:
"The Lord has risen!
All hail, the King!
Stone, stone roll away,
This is Resurrection day!"

*... Ye seek Jesus of Nazareth,
which was crucified: He is risen;
He is not here. Mark 16:6*

THOUSANDS OF ANGELS

Thousands of angels
Followed The Lord,
As He made everything that was good;
Thousands of angels followed The Lord,
As He walked in sweet Eden's wood.

Thousands of angels
Followed The Lord,
When He came as a Babe to the earth.
Thousands of angels followed and sang
On the night of The Savior's birth!

Thousands of angels
Followed The Lord,
As He taught, as He healed, as He blessed;
Thousands of angels followed The Lord,
As He walked in the wilderness.

But, there on the Cross
The Lord was alone;
No angel could follow Him there.
Alone, through His love for you and me,
He suffered what no one could share.

And then shall He send His angels,
and shall gather together His elect
from the four winds.   Mark 13:27

But He is alive!
And back from the dead!
And thousands of angels, once more,
Will follow the Lord to bring His lambs
To live with Him evermore!

JESUS' FAMILY ALBUM

There are many books in Heaven,
    And we'll see them all, someday.
God will show us His great library,
    That He has stored away.
And, oh! the wonders we shall find,
    Inside those Heavenly pages.
But Jesus has one special Book,
    That's grown throughout the ages.

It's Jesus' Family Album;
    Every name is written there,
Of those who are His children,
    All those names from everywhere!
And when we get to Heaven,
    And go through those pearly doors,
In Jesus' Family Album,
    I hope mine is next to yours!

JESUS LOVES ME

Jesus loves me, as I am;
He's my Shepherd, I'm His lamb.
He will keep me safe each day,
In His loving Savior way.

Jesus loves me, and His love
Leads me up to Heaven above.
There, someday, I'll see His face,
In that shining, happy place.

I am the good Shepherd: the good
Shepherd giveth His life for the sheep.
John 10:11

I'M A FRIEND OF JESUS

I'm a friend of Jesus,
  Although I'm very small.
He called me His dear friend
Because I love Him
Best of all.
I know He is my Savior,
And I know He's God divine;
But it's so wonderful
That I'm His friend,
And He is mine!

... I have called you friends.
John 15:15

LITTLE THINGS

A little mustard seed can grow
    A mighty mustard tree;
A home where all the birds can nest,
    And raise a family.
A mustard home! Indeed, birds need
    That tiny, little mustard seed.

A little heart can quite believe
    In Jesus, God's dear Son.
And grow to show His love and power,
    And grace to everyone.
A child of God! Oh, see your part!
    We all need your believing heart.

WATCHING CLOUDS

I love to watch the fluffy clouds
    Make pictures in the sky.
They're like a moving picture book,
    That changes as I spy!

Sometimes I see big elephants,
    That change to kangaroos;
And even woolly lambs that walk
    Across the skies in shoes!

Sometimes I see a sailing ship,
    Or miles of angels' wings;
I've even seen the flags all fly
    On castles of the kings!

But one cloud I am watching for
    Especially to appear ...
The one that when God's trumpet blows,
    Will bring The Lord back here!

The heavens declare the glory of God ... Psalm 19:1

GOD'S GOODNESS SHINES

If stars came out just once a year,
We'd wait to see the stars appear!
We'd gasp, and watch their twinkling light,
And stay up watching through the night!
But God is good and every night
He gives us stars for our delight.
And dotted there, in diamond skies,
God's goodness shines in starry eyes.

BREAKFAST WITH THE KING

Seven hungry fishermen
　　Went fishing through the night;
Hoping they would fill their net,
　　Before the morning light.

Working hard together,
　　They cast their net, "Swish, swish."
Their net caught sparkling moonbeams,
　　But not a single fish!

Seven hungry fishermen,
　　Were hungrier than ever.
The night was gone; the sun was up;
　　The fish had been too clever!

Then, all at once, they heard a shout
　　From Someone on the shore:
"Have you any fish, my friends?"
　　"No! Not a fish in store."

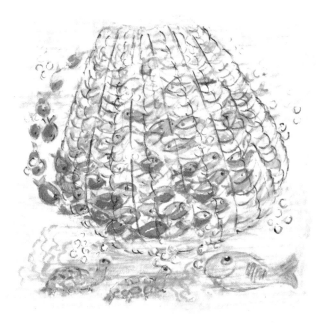

"Then, cast your net off to the right;
    That's where the fish will be."
So seven hungry fishermen
    Cast out again to sea.

One hundred, fifty, plus three more,
    Large fish of every sort,
Packed the bulging net, as if
    They wanted to be caught.

They pulled the bulging net of fish,
　　That couldn't hold one more.
They knew that miracle of fish
　　Was from the 'One' on shore.

"It is the Lord! The risen Lord!"
　　They shouted happily.
"We'll count our blessings here today;
　　One hundred fifty three!"

"Come, now, to breakfast," Jesus said,
　　"There's fish for all to eat."
Then Jesus served them, one by one,
　　A tasty breakfast treat.

When they were full, the seven sat
　　Astonished! Wondering...
The risen Lord, Himself, had served
　　Their breakfast with The King.

THE DOOR

I like the door to our house,
  And the door up on the hill;
And the doors across the meadow,
  Leading past the old windmill.
But there's a door to Heaven
  That I love the very best,
Because the Door is Jesus,
  Who loves every little guest.

Ride a white horse,
And pray for the day
Jesus will ride
From Heaven's highway!

Dressed in a robe
Of glorious red;
A mighty Warrior,
With a crown on His head!

Down through the clouds,
And over the sky;
Proclaiming His Name
From Heaven on high:

And I saw heaven opened, and
behold a white horse ....
Rev. 19:11

"LORD OF ALL LORDS,
    AND KING OF ALL KINGS!"
Rejoice! little children!
    Come, join in and sing ...

Ride a white horse,
    And pray for the day
Jesus will ride
    From Heaven's highway!

IF ALL THAT JESUS DID

f all the things
That Jesus did
Were written down
On pages,
The whole wide world
Could never hold
What He's done
Throughout the ages!

And there are also many other things
which Jesus did ... that even the world
itself could not contain the books that
should be written.
John 21:25

... Who went about doing good.
Acts 10:38

JESUS WENT ABOUT DOING GOOD

Up the streets,
Down the streets,
'Round the neighborhood.
Up the hills,
Down the hills,
Always doing good.
All along the seashore,
Through the fields and wood,
Our Lord Jesus went about
Always doing good.

Marjorie Ainsborough Decker

Marjorie Decker, ECPA Gold Award Winner, is a #1 National Bestseller author, well-known and loved for her distinct story-telling style.

A native of Liverpool, England, Marjorie resides in the United States with her husband, Dale. They are the parents of four grown sons. Her Christian Mother Goose® Classics have endeared the trust of parents and grandparents, and the twinkle of children world-wide.

Along with authoring many books in the Christian Mother Goose® Series, Marjorie brings fresh enthusiasm and dynamic teaching to sound, Biblical scholarship. There is a pleasant nostalgia to her children's books with a curious appeal to Bible lovers of all ages.

Recognized by the Christian Booksellers Association as one of the "Top Ten Bestselling Authors of The Decade," Mrs. Decker is also a frequent guest of national radio and television, a recording artist and popular conference speaker.